Bracelet Crafting Book

Master the Art of Basic Craft with Step by Step Instructions

Honey R Orson

Table of Contents

WHAT IS A SURVIVAL BRACELET?

A survival bracelet can be very simple, using only cord, or it can be quite complicated using a variety of findings, cord, gadgets and attachments. In theory a survival bracelet at a minimum is made from 550 paracord. The entire bracelet should be able to be untied, taken apart, and used in various emergency situations. The idea here is that if you are wearing the bracelet at all times, and the need arises, then you have yourself an emergency source of cord (and possibly other survival goodies) should a survival situation arise.

For example, a survival bracelets inner strands can be removed and used for fishing line, snares, shelter construction, fire starting, tourniquets and emergency shoe laces to name just a few of the possible applications. More complicated verities of survival bracelets can be made that incorporate medic alert tags, dog tags, bottle opener, flint and steel, fishing line, snare wire, fancy connecting devices and even watches.

More realistically, a survival bracelet is a "tacticool" fashion accessory that will never get used for any emergency situation. I haven't even heard of a story where a survival bracelet was used in an emergency. There is a humorous demonstration of a survival strap in use by Steve Austin in the movie "Hunt To Kill". In that movie, he takes his fancy survival bracelet apart and uses it to rappel off of a cliff. That may not be a very realistic use of a survival bracelet, but the movie was worth a look anyway.

Personally, I really like my survival bracelets and I enjoy wearing them. I frequently get compliments on my survival bracelet watch band, which I wear nearly every day. Not only that, but I also enjoy telling the person complementing me that "I made that" bracelet. I like to keep a few bracelets with me when I leave the house to showcase my skills just in case anyone shows some interest. I have made more than one sale that way.

I spent several years working around the globe as a soldier in the US Army. During that time, we used paracord daily for hundreds of applications. For several years after my military service ended, I worked as a contractor for the U.S Army. As such, I have made some cash in my spare time each day making simple paracord projects for the soldiers. When I sell to soldiers, I sell them my paracord projects at fifty percent off my regular prices. So, even at discounted prices there is the potential to make money doing this type of work if you have the talent for it and enjoy knot tying as much as I do.

A fashionable survival strap can be made from just about any kind of cord or other types of paracord. However, for it to be a truly functional survival strap, it should be made from 550 paracord.

Only a short length of paracord will be needed for the project outlined in this eBook. Only 10' of paracord or less is what you will need.

Figure 1 You can make a Survival Strap just like this one!

WHAT IS PARACORD?

In the beginning, 550 cord (AKA paracord) was in use by the US Army. The Army used paracord for suspension lines in parachutes during WWII. Paracord is now widely available to all branches of the military and is obviously produced for civilian use as well. The "550" part of the common paracord name refers to the design specification that the cord should have a minimum breaking strength of 550 pounds. Additionally, paracord was designed to stretch 30%. Like many cords and ropes that are made from synthetic material and are woven, paracord is made with a woven synthetic sheath (specifically nylon). It is unofficially understood that 550 paracord has the thickness of 5/32". The hollow outer sheath contains with in it seven strands of two-ply string or yarn. Some advantages of paracord are that it is very resistant to mildew and rot and it is also stretchable. Paracord is also resistant to wear and UV damage. Because of this, paracord will stay looking great and working as designed for years when properly cared for.

Figure 1. This picture shows the seven inner strands of two-ply paracord, surrounded by the outer (orange color) braided nylon

sheath. I untwisted the two-ply strand on the left side so that you can see what the real paracord inner strands are supposed to look like.

It's easy to test your cord to see if it's real 550 paracord. Take a look at an open end of the cord, pick out and count the inner strands, if there are any. Real 550 paracord will have 7 inner strands of two-ply string in the middle of the hollow sheath that are easily removable.

This feature lends another dimension to working with 550 paracord. When making the same projects with or without the 7 strands in the middle of your paracord will make a drastic difference in the appearance, strength and even in the way you will be able to use the item when it's finished. In short, the seven inner strands in paracord reinforce the cord. When the seven inner strands are removed, paracord can be an interesting and fun way to make projects so they have a different look and feel to them.

HOW TO ACQUIRE PARACORD

These days paracord is fairly easy to find, you may even be able to find it at stores in your area right now! Try to find it at sporting goods stores or the sporting goods section in larger stores. I have found paracord for sale at western supply houses, sporting goods stores, Army surplus stores, military "clothing and sales" stores and gun shows. They even sell paracord at my local Walmart store. I have found paracord in both the sporting goods section where the camping equipment is and in the hobby section where the other cord and string are located.

A note of caution though, is that the cord I have bought at Walmart is sometimes not real 550 paracord with the seven two-ply strands inside. I have even bought paracord there that says it has seven inner strands, but was disappointed when I got home and cut the paracord open to find the inner seven strands were actually just a filler of some kind.

If the previous tips above don't work to get some paracord in your hands you can always try the internet. That crazy internet has just about everything you could ever want! Simply pull up your favorite internet browser and navigate to a search engine like Google. Search for "550 paracord 7 inner strands". You should get thousands of results from that search query. While clicking the links, compare prices from different websites and be sure that the cord you buy is called 550 cord or paracord. Even then the cord you get may not be real 550 cord. Remember, unless it has the 7 inner two-ply strands, it is not real 550 paracord. I usually look for the "7 inner strands" or similar description in the product information. If you can't find 550 cord that has a description as having 7 inner strands, you can email or contact the website that has the paracord for sale to confirm that you are getting real 550 paracord. Or, you can click this link...

PARACORD PLANET Paracord (50+ Colors) - 1,000 Foot spools - 250 Foot spools - 100 feet Hank

You should be able to get just about any color you can think of in 550 cord these days. And you can get it in lengths from 50' to 1000' rolls. You don't need to go crazy your first time. I recommend getting a hank of 100' in whatever color or colors you like to get started.

If for some reason you are unable to find real 550 paracord. Don't let that stop you from getting started. You can make survival bracelets out of just about any cord, string or small diameters of rope. The project we will make is suited to all these types of cord, string and rope. Even a beginner should be able to make this project in under an hour.

WORKING WITH PARACORD

Ok, we have discussed what a survival bracelet is. Hopefully you have acquired some paracord or similar cordage to work with. Now it is time to learn some of the basic qualities of paracord. After that, we will have a brief discussion of the techniques we will be using. And then finally we will get to work on making that survival bracelet that I have been telling you about.

Estimating Cord Length

This is a tricky skill to learn. It is even trickier to properly explain to someone, but I will give it my best try. Even today, after all my years of doing knot work, I still sometimes make mistakes and start a project with too little or too much cord. Don't be discouraged if you get the cord length wrong. Just take the project apart and save the cord for something you make in the future. It is virtually always better to have cut the cord too long than 95too short.

Here are some things that can affect the length of cord that you will need. Cord circumference (if you are using paracord, disregard this), project length & cord shrinkage (yes, paracord will shrink a bit). For the project we will be making, cord shrinkage will not be a factor as the finished project will be somewhat adjustable.

My rule of thumb for estimating the length of a Solomon bar knot (we will learn to tie this knot later) is to figure out the length of the finished project. In our case it will be the circumference of the wrist that your bracelet will be worn on. In order, here are the steps you need to take to estimate your cord length.

1. Measure the circumference of the wrist that the bracelet will be worn on. You can use a tape measure or ruler, but the

easiest way I have found is to wrap a length of cord around my wrist and measure that.

2. Multiply the number you got in step #1 by 12.

That is all you really need to do.   Using my wrist as an example, the circumference of my wrist is about 7 ¼". We multiply that measurement times 12 which gives us a total of 87" or just a bit longer than seven feet. I'm going to add another 18 inches to the total, just to be sure there is enough cord to finish the project. That will give me a total of 95" of paracord.

Tying the knots

When tying the knots, one of the most important things to remember is to keep the tension even throughout the knot-tying process. For example, if you start your bracelet off with a very tight knot and finish it with a loose not, the tight end will be compact and stiff compared to the loose end, which will be softer and more flexible.

Either way you tie the knot is fine. Both ways have advantages and disadvantages. Whichever way you tie your knot, remember, the key to having a professional finished product to have consistent tension when working the cord and pulling the knots tight, throughout the process.

KNOT TERMINOLOGY

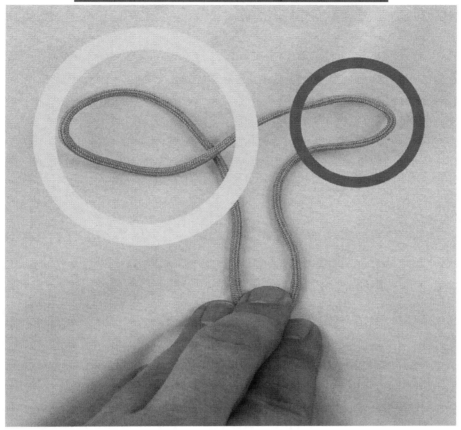

Figure 2 shows a loop circled in yellow and a bight circled in red

We will now go over some knot tying terminology so that you can understand the basic concepts of knot tying. It is important to know the difference between a loop and a bight.

A loop is a length of cord, twine, rope, cable, etc., that forms a curve and then eventually curves back across itself. Figure 2.1 shows a loop circled in yellow.

A bight is a length of cord that will bend back forming a "U" shape, but it doesn't cross back over itself. Figure 2.1 above shows a bight circled in red.

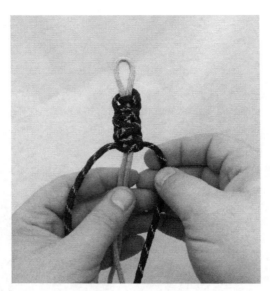

Figure 3. in this example, the coyote brown cords in the middle of the knot are the "filler cords," the black cord with the reflective stripes is being used as the "working ends" of the knot.

The "working ends" of a cord are the ends that you will actually be doing the knot tying with. There will be two center strands of cord that we will use in this project. We won't use those strands to tie any knots with for the project itself. Those cords are called the "filler cords."

Whipping your paracord

When you cut a piece of cord off of a hank or spool of paracord, you will want to apply a whipping to the ends of the cord. This will help the ends of your paracord from fraying. Additionally, it will help the internal strands from bunching up inside the outer sheath of the paracord.

There are many types of whippings. The only real practical whipping for paracord is sewing or melting the ends. Most people who work with paracord use fire to melt the ends of the cord. This is a quick and efficient way to prevent fraying. There are several techniques to apply the whipping on paracord. We will go over a basic whipping now.

The whipping I will teach you is the type where you melt the ends. This process has advantages and disadvantages. The advantage is that it is a quick and easy way to prevent the severed cord ends from unraveling. Some disadvantages are that once you shape the melted end, it is pretty much stuck that way forever. If you want to do a different whipping, or redo you current whipping, you have to cut the old one off and start again. Just remember that and you will be fine.

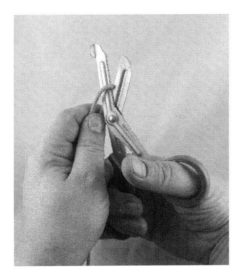

1. Cut the cord cleanly with a sharp knife or scissors, being very careful to not cut yourself

2. Being careful to not burn yourself, bring a flame close to the freshly cut end of the cord, until it is just barely touching the end of

the cord

2. When the cord starts to bubble and turn black, it is singed enough. Extinguish the flame at this point

If the cord has caught on fire, carefully blow it out the fire. Be very careful, the melted part of the paracord is VERY hot and if you touch it, it will burn you until it has cooled off.

If you hold the cord vertically with the singed end up, it will form a small roundish ball of melted cord on top. The cord will cool quickly (thirty seconds at most), but you may gently blow on it to speed up the cooling process

TYING THE SOLOMON BAR

And now we come to the moment of truth. After being patient and reading through to this part, you will now be rewarded with the payoff. Before we get stared with the instructions for making the survival bracelet, let's take a few moments to prepare.

First, find an area with appropriate space and lighting so that you can see what you are doing. Secondly, gather all your materials. At a minimum you will need several feet of cordage, a cutting instrument such as a knife or a nice sharp pair of scissors and lastly you will need a source of fire. When I am doing knot work, I cut my cord with scissors and melt the ends with a regular butane lighter. A knife may be used to cut your paracord. Some knives work better than others for this task. On occasion, when doing complicated work where I don't want to let go of the paracord to melt the ends, I have used a candle to apply a whipping with satisfactory results.

I want you to remember that there are many different techniques to tie the same knot. I will teach you the method that works best for me. You may have opportunities to learn different methods later. Pay attention when this happens, because you may learn a new way to tie the same knot that works better for you. Additionally, it is common for the same knot to have many names. I don't want you to be confused when you learn to tie the "larks head hitch" and later on down the road in your knot tying adventures, someone tries to teach you how to tie the "Bale Sling hitch, Baggage Tag Loop, Cow hitch, Deadeye hitch, Girth hitch, Lanyard hitch, Lark's foot, Ring hitch or the Tag Knot," and you discover it is the same knot.

A brief safety note will be mentioned here. Please do not hurt yourself with sharp objects or fire. If you are very young or for some reason you need help with this project, please seek out assistance before getting started. I have been doing this kind of work for 20 over years, and I still cut myself, poke myself with needles and burn my fingers on molten hot cord from time to time. PLEASE be careful.

LET'S GET STARTED

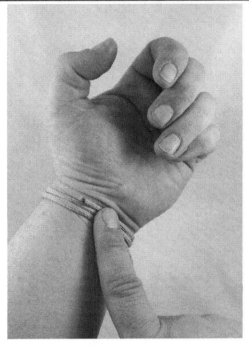

Figure 4. In this illustration, I have only made two wraps around my wrist, and not the required four wraps.

　　1.　Cut a piece of paracord to be used as the filler cord.　It should be the circumference of your wrist times four.　Be sure to melt the ends of the cord that you have just cut to prevent them from fraying. Click here for instructions

　　2.　Cut the proper length of cord for the working ends of your Solomon bar knot as described under the "Working with Paracord" chapter, under the subheading of "Estimating cord length"

　　3.　Find the middle of your working cord by folding it in half and place the middle of the cord on a flat surface with the middle of the cord held horizontally

　　4.　Fold the filler cord in half so that the ends are together and the middle of the cord forms a bight

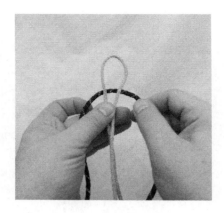

5. Lay the Filler cord over the top of the middle of your working ends of cord so that the bight end of the filler cord is pointing upwards

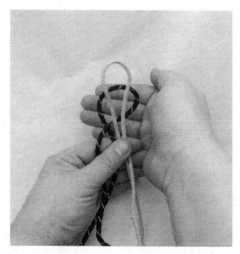

Figure 5. When done properly a small bight is formed on the right side of the filler cords in this step

6. Fold the working end on the right side under the filler cords and then over the top of the working end on the left side. When done properly, a small bight is formed on the right side of the filler cords

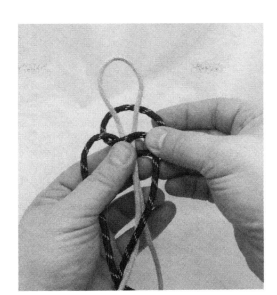

7. Fold the working end of the cord that was on the left side of the filler cord first (it's also the working cord that you crossed over in step #6) over the filler cords

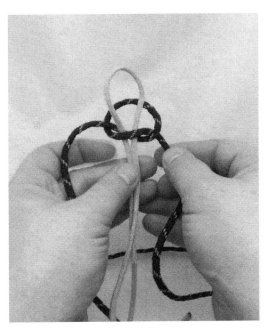

8. Push the same working end down through the bight formed on the right side of the filler cords step # 6

9. Pull on both ends of the working cords and pull the knot snug down against the filler cords, leaving about a one inch bight of filler cord sticking out of the top.

NOTE Now, we will repeat that same process we just did, however, this time, start your knot tying on the left hand side

10. Fold the working end on the left hand side of the filler cords under the filler cords and over the working end on the right side. This should form a small bight of working cord under the filler cords on the left hand side of the knot.

11. Fold the working end that was on the right side of the filler cords first, in step #9 over the working cords

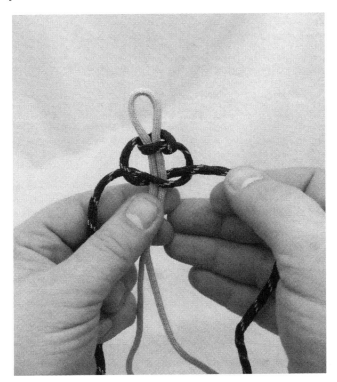

12. Push the same working end through the bight created in step #10

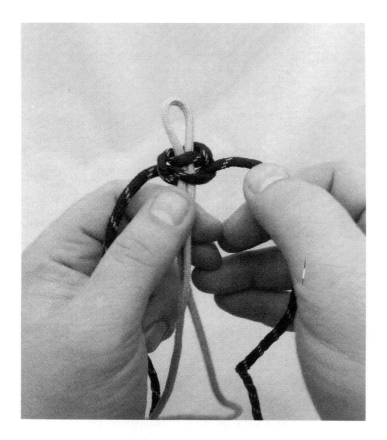

13. Pull the working ends so that you will snug up the knot to the filler cords

14. Repeat steps #1 through #13 until your Solomon Bar is the desired length

15. Remember to keep even tension on the knots as you pull them snug up next to the filler cords so that your finished product will have an even appearance and feel to it

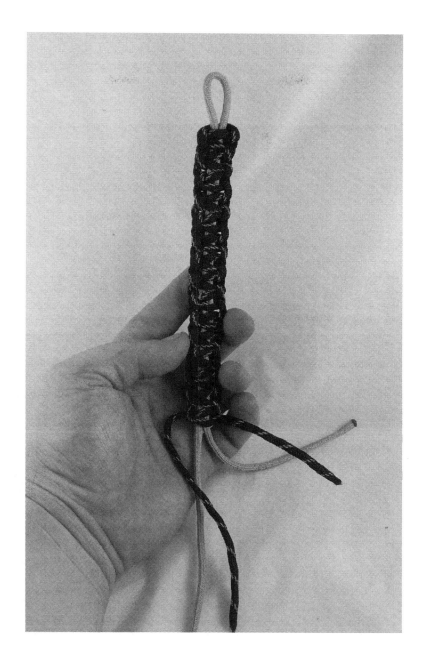

16. Continue tying the knots on your filler cords until you run out of working cord ends or until the bracelet will fit around your wrist

17. Tie the final knot as tight as you can get it

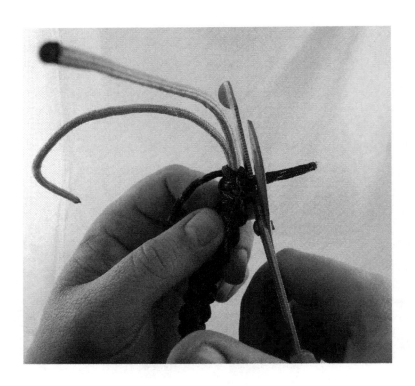

18. Cut one of the working ends so that only about 1/8" of cord is sticking up from the knot

19. Hold the bracelet with the stub of paracord sticking out to the side or straight up.

20. Use fire to melt the cord until it is a blackened melting blob

21. Remove the fire from the knot and hold it so that the hot melting blob is pointing upwards for about 15 seconds. Blow out the flame if there is any

22. Repeat steps #18 through step #21 on the other working end

23. After you have melted the end and your first Solomon bar is completed

Next I will teach you how to attach the bracelet to your wrist using a square knot.

TYING THE SQUARE KNOT

Tying a square knot is really simple once you get the hang of it. I use this knot quite a bit. It is a handy knot to know as it is fairly easy to untie and once it is tied down properly, it will not easily come untied on its own. Depending on the technique you use to tie your shoes, you already know half of the knot. It starts off as a granny knot, also known as an overhand knot. If you are in martial arts, the square knot is the same knot you use to tie your belt on with.

For our purposes, we will be tying the knot using the filler cord ends and bight. The filler cord ends will now become the working ends as we tie the square knot through the filler cords bight.

1. Wrap the bracelet around your wrist

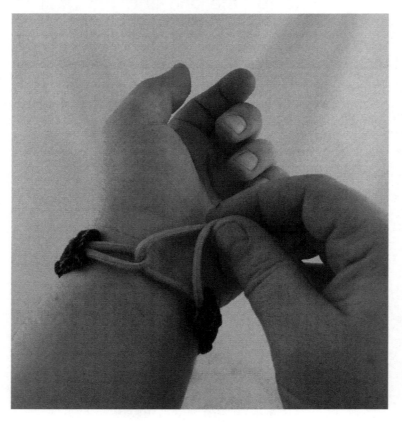

2. Wrap one of the working ends up through the filler cord bight
3. Fold the other working end in front of the working end that went through the bight in step #2

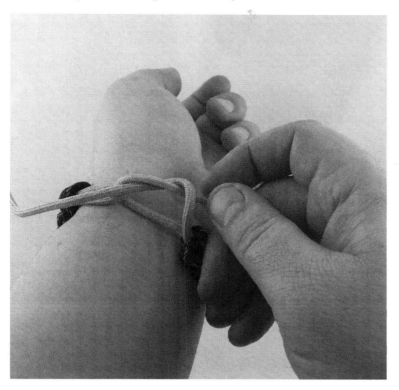

4. Continue wrapping that working end around the other working end until it completely goes around it and comes out the same side it went in on

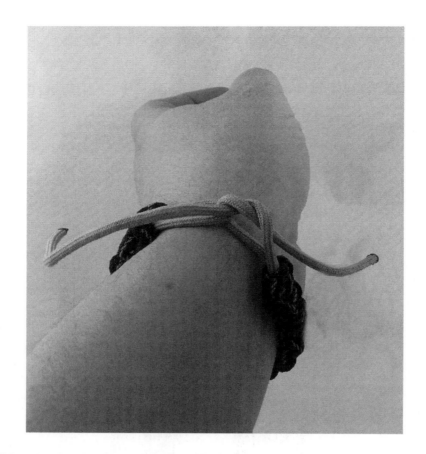

5. Cinch down the knot, but don't get it too tight. You want to leave a little slack so that the bracelet is comfortable on your wrist.

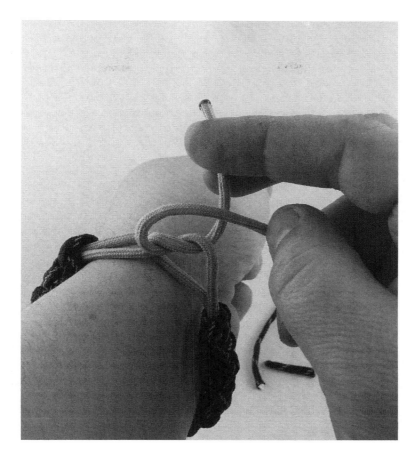

6. Now tie another overhand knot, but this time cross the working end on the left side in front of the other working end

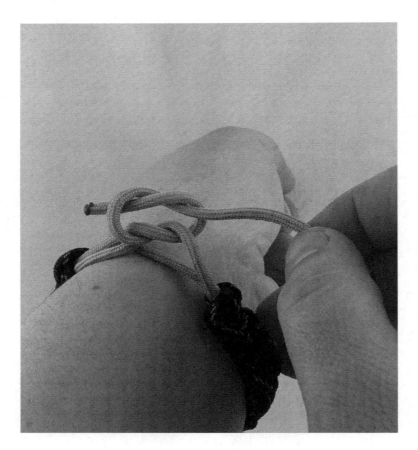

7. Continue wrapping the left working end around the right working end until it completely goes around it and comes out the same side it went in on.

8. Pull the knot tight, but not too tight, as you will want to untie it again later when you decide to take it off. I usually use my free hand and my teeth to pull the knot tight.

Figure 6. I like to be able to easily fit a couple fingers under the bracelet after I have it secured to my wrist. That is about the right fit for me.

ADVANCED TECHNIQUES

This chapter of my eBook will provide you with food for thought regarding future projects you may wish to try. Additionally, these will be some of the topics that I will cover in greater detail in my follow-up eBook.

Findings:

There are several ways to connect the ends of the finished survival strap together without tying the working ends together. In my follow-up eBook, I will cover about half a dozen different ways that you can easily and quickly connect the ends of your survival strap. For example we will cover using side release buckles, different kinds of buttons, cord locks and more.

Figure 7. These are some of the findings that I use in my paracord work. The top row are various types of cord locks. In the middle left is an adjustable length buckle that I use for bracelets. Middle right are two large buttons salvaged from used military battle uniforms. The bottom row are side release buckles of different sizes for

survival bracelets. The orange and black and off-white colored buckles also have a whistle built in.

Splicing:

There are times when you may want to join two pieces of cord together for a variety of reasons. I know a few methods that will give a fairly clean and smooth transition in the splicing process. In my follow-up eBook, I will share these tips and techniques with you.

Paracord tools:

For years I considered myself a minimalist in the genre of knot-tying. The only tools I used were my trusty pocket knife, needle, thread, lighter and an awl. What is an awl you may ask? An awl is a tool that is used while tying knots to helps create space in areas where the knot is already tied or is being tied so that you can push your paracord through. Or you can use the awl to just push the paracord through the knot. An awl is a very handy tool to have. I still have the very first awl that was given to me, and I still use it.

Making a serviceable awl yourself is a fairly easy process if you have the right tools and supplies. I will walk you through this procedure in a follow-up eBook. Additionally, I will cover several other tools that I use to speed up my knot tying time and to give the whole project a more professional appearance. All the tools you need for working paracord can be kept in a container such as a small bag. If you want to get really fancy, all the tools you should need for working paracord could be held in the <u>same small pouch that I use</u>.

Improvising

One lesson I hope to teach future eBooks, is how to look at a project and decide what improvements or changes can be made to it and then implementing a plan to carry out those changes. Admittedly this is a skill that is easier to learn than it is to teach. My goal here will be to teach you the many different ways that a survival strap can be tied using various modifications of the modest Solomon

Bar. Hopefully this will fuel your creative processes and get you thinking about how simple changes can make big differences in the appearance or use of the finished product.

Other Knots

Even though I want to write a follow-up eBook with several new styles of survival bracelets using only slight modifications of the Solomon bar, I still intend to teach several new knots in the new eBook. Some of the knots that are likely to be covered are the diamond knot. Knots that I call the simple Solomon, king knot, advanced Solomon, chain Solomon, Solomon's ladder and Solomon fringe.

Finishing

Another advanced technique is to learn to hide the ends of your project. When done properly, it is nearly impossible to see the ends of the cords. This makes your knotting work look much more professional and uniform.

Real Uses for a survival bracelet

I also intend to write about real things that you can do with the survival bracelet if you ever find yourself in an emergency situation. A lot of instruction out there exists for how to make a bracelet. But there isn't a lot of instruction on how to use the bracelet in a "survival" situation, even if you have one in your possession when a survival scenario unfolds. I will provide some information and ideas for uses of the survival bracelet if you are ever unfortunate enough to get into a survival situation. Which is really the idea behind a "survival" bracelet.

GLOSSARY

550 Paracord	Cordage made from nylon consisting of an outer braided sheath that contains seven inner strand of two-ply string.
Awl	A tool with a pointed end used for widening or creating holes or openings which other objects may pass through.
Bar	A series of knots tied in such a way as to form a long flattish finished knot work design. For example a bar tied long and wide enough would make a fine belt, a decorative cover for a backpack strap and so on.
Bight	A bight is a length of cord that will bend back forming a "U" shape, but doesn't cross back over itself.
Circumference	The total distance measured around the outside of a circle or other similar shaped object.
Fid	A rigid needle-like tool with a sharp point on one end and the other end has a female treaded receptor that you can "screw" your paracord into forming a sort of needle and thread like set-up
Fray	Coming apart or loosening
Hank	A specific length of yarn, twine, string, cord or rope looped or coiled about itself for a convenient way to carry it without tangling.
Knot	A length of any flexible material, usually yarn, string, cord, rope or cable wrapped or tangled around itself or other materials in such a way as to form a lump in the flexible material used.
Loop	A length of cord, twine, rope, cable, etc., that forms a curve and then eventually curves back across itself.
Nylon	Any textile formed out of a synthetic polyamide material which is flexible and flexible such as thread, twine, string, cord or rope.
Paracord	A length of braided nylon cordage used in the manufacture of parachute lines.

Paracord findings	Any number of beads, trinkets, fastening items or gizmos used when making craft items out of paracord.
Rope	A thick twisted or braided length of flexible material made up of other fibers, cords, strings or yarn.
Shears	A hand-held cutting tool similar to scissors that are heavy-duty and usually designed for a specific purpose.
Sheath	An outer covering designed to protect the contents.
Solomon Bar	A series of repeating square knots tied around a filler item such as a rigid pole or cordage.
Splice	Two or more pieces of rope, cord or sting joined together by means of braiding tying or weaving.
Spool	A device used for wrapping thread, twine, string, cord or rope in such a way that the cord has to be unwound from the spool to remove it.
String	Two or more lengths of material made from synthetic or natural materials usually twisted or braided together, sometimes used to manufacture cord or rope.
Survival Bracelet	A bracelet made from paracord that is easy to untie so that you have a length of cordage in a "survival" situation.
Survival Strap	See the "Survival Bracelet" entry.
Synthetic	Artificial materials not found in nature.
Two-ply	Two items joined together usually for the purpose of strengthening the material in some way.
Whipping	Finishing the ends of string, cord or rope in such a way as to prevent the cord from unraveling.
Working Ends	The end(s) of cord, string, twine or rope that are used to tie knots.
Yarn	A long even strand of material that is used to make materials, cordage string or rope.
Zipper pull	The part of a zipper that you grab onto in order to open or close the zipper.

Printed in Great Britain
by Amazon